Fortune Fav...

BOLD

from SmarterComics

WRITTEN BY
FRANCO ARDA

ILLUSTRATED BY
ANJIN ANHUT

Fortune Favors the BOLD

from SmarterComics

Franco Arda   Author

Anjin Anhut   Illustrator

Sander Pieterse   Designer

Jennifer Kunz   Creative Director

Published by SmarterComics, LLC, Palo Alto, CA 95054, United States of America

www.SmarterComics.com

ISBN-13: 978-1-61082-995-3

DISCLAIMER

This book provides ideas to lead a bold life. This is not advice. Use it at your own risk. I do not take responsibility for rashes, financial ruin, or any other misfortune - either directly or indirectly - from applying the ideas in this book.

ACKNOWLEDGEMENT

Many of the ideas presented here were inspired by great leaders, athletes, movies and authors. For a complete list of those who helped jumpstart my own bold thought process, see Notes & References at the end of the book.

Dedicated to Joelina Arda

(born September 24, 2007 - Hong Kong)

It is your father's obligation to leave you with a deeply rooted understanding that life is a spectacular adventure to be embraced.

Love, Daddy

INTRODUCTION

My experience has taught me that boldness is not the secret of success, but it is an essential ingredient in becoming successful.

What is boldness exactly? **Boldness is the willingness to make things happen, despite the risks.** It is broadly synonymous with bravery and courage, but includes one extra, necessary element: ACTION.

Being bold is not the same as being aggressive. You do not need to actively impress your opinions on others in order to be bold. Instead, **you must actively face your fears and barrel through them.**

Of course, being bold is not about taking unnecessary risk or engaging in reckless or illegal behavior.

Boldness is not waiting for opportunities; it is creating them.

Boldness, when embraced, leverages all of our other abilities. It invokes within us our best selves.

Franco Arda
Berlin 2010

TABLE OF CONTENTS

LIVE YOUR DREAMS 1

YOUR DAYS ARE NUMBERED 3

LIFE IS RISKY 5

ACCEPT YOUR FEARS, BUT DO IT ANYWAY 7

BOLD ACTION OR NO ACTION 9

LIFE LESSONS FROM POKER 11

LIFE LESSONS FROM SKIING 13

CONFIDENCE = BELIEVING IN YOURSELF 15

A MILLION DOLLAR$ 17

BE DIFFERENT OR BE AVERAGE 19

STRATEGY vs. TACTICS 21

FOCUS + SPEED = MOMENTUM 23

THE AVERAGE NEVER WINS 25

PRISON BREAK 27

CONFIDENCE PRECEDES SUCCESS 29

IT'S OK TO FAIL 31

DARE TO BE DIFFERENT 33

LIFE'S A (SMART) GAMBLE 35

INTELLIGENCE IS OVERRATED 37

IGNORANCE CAN BE SMART 39

BOLD DECISIONS 41

HIGH–STAKES NEGOTIATIONS 43

THINK TWICE, BUT GO WITH YOUR GUT 45

MAKE LUCK WORK FOR YOU 47

GO FOR A HOME RUN 49

CHAPTER 1:
LIVE YOUR DREAMS

"THE BIGGEST ADVENTURE YOU CAN TAKE IS TO LIVE THE LIFE OF YOUR DREAMS." - OPRAH WINFREY

AS WE ENTER ADULTHOOD, SO MANY OF US FIND OURSELVES TOO SCARED TO FOLLOW THE DREAMS OF OUR PAST.

WE OFTEN FORGET THAT DREAMS ARE THE FUEL THAT DRIVES THE ENGINE OF OUR LIVES...

...A THRILL WE CAN FEEL EVERY DAY IF WE PURSUE SOMETHING THAT GIVES US REAL MEANING.

NO MATTER HOW BIG YOUR DREAM IS...
NO MATTER HOW IMPOSSIBLE YOUR DREAM IS...
NO MATTER WHAT OTHER PEOPLE THINK ABOUT YOUR DREAM...

IF YOU CAN BELIEVE YOUR DREAM IS POSSIBLE, YOUR MIND WILL GO TO WORK AND FIND THE WAYS TO ACHIEVE IT.

2

CHAPTER 2: YOUR DAYS ARE NUMBERED

"DON'T ACT AS THOUGH YOU'LL LIVE TO BE A THOUSAND YEARS. YOUR DAYS ARE NUMBERED LIKE EVERYONE ELSE'S."
– MARCUS AURELIUS

LIFE IS SHORT.

BY THE TIME MOST OF US BECOME EVEN A LITTLE WISE, 40 YEARS HAVE GONE BY.

ANOTHER 40 YEARS FROM THERE, AND YOU'LL PROBABLY BE GONE, TOO!

REMIND YOURSELF OF THE SHORTNESS OF LIFE. THIS CAN HAVE A VERY POSITIVE EFFECT ON YOUR TIME HERE.

THE END

DEVELOP A SENSE OF URGENCY, AND NURTURE A MISSION THROUGHOUT YOUR LIFE.

ACHIEVE SPEED WITHOUT HASTE. THERE IS A GREAT DIFFERENCE BETWEEN THESE TWO WORDS.

OF COURSE, IT'S RIDICULOUS TO WORRY ABOUT SPEED BEFORE DIRECTION. THAT'S PRECISELY WHY YOU NEED TO BEGIN WITH YOUR DREAM.

popcorn

now playing:

now playing:

"THE SADDEST SUMMARY OF A LIFE MIGHT CONTAIN ANY OF THE FOLLOWING: COULD HAVE, MIGHT HAVE, SHOULD HAVE."
-UNKOWN

CHAPTER 3:
LIFE IS RISKY

*"BE WILLING TO TAKE A RISK.
REMEMBER, THERE IS NO SECURITY IN
LIFE. THERE IS ONLY ADVENTURE."
- GARY MACK*

ALL COURSES OF
ACTION ARE RISKY.

AVOIDING DANGER
IS IMPOSSIBLE.

YOU MUST PURSUE
OPPORTUNITIES
THAT DON'T WORK
OUT WELL.

IF YOU NEVER TRY
AT ALL, YOU MAKE IT
IMPOSSIBLE TO
SUCCEED.

BOLDNESS IS ALWAYS
EXPRESSED IN THE WILLINGNESS TO
MOVE FORWARD WITH DETERMINATION,
TO FACE DANGER, TO TAKE RISKS...

...WITHOUT THE GUARANTEE OF SUCCESS.

DAVID VISCOTT, AN AMERICAN PSYCHIATRIST, SAID: "THE DRIVER MOST LIKELY TO BE KILLED IS THE ONE WHO HESITATES, LOSES HIS NERVE, AND CAN NEITHER ACCELERATE NOR APPLY HIS BRAKES."

BE BOLD. DON'T LET DANGER STOP YOU FROM DOING GREAT THINGS.

CHAPTER 4:
ACCEPT YOUR FEARS,
BUT DO IT ANYWAY

*"IF YOU DON'T CONTROL YOUR
FEAR, FEAR CONTROLS YOU."*
- TOM HOPKINS

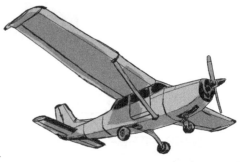

FEAR IS THE MOST
POWERFUL ENEMY
OF SUCCESS.

FEAR OF FAILURE OFTEN
PREVENTS PEOPLE FROM
ACHIEVING GREATNESS.

BUT FEARLESSNESS IS NOT
THE ANSWER -
FEARLESSNESS LEADS TO
RECKLESSNESS.

THERE IS A TIME TO LISTEN
TO YOUR FEARS, AND THERE IS
A TIME TO PUSH THEM ASIDE.

CHAPTER 5:
BOLD ACTION OR
NO ACTION

"DO OR DO NOT. THERE IS NO TRY"
-YODA IN STAR WARS

HESITATION CAN
BE DANGEROUS.

PROCEED WITH
BOLDNESS.

ACT BOLDLY
OR DON'T ACT
AT ALL.

HESITATION AND BOLDNESS
HAVE DIFFERENT
PSYCHOLOGICAL AND PHYSICAL
RESPONSES:

HESITATION
ATTRACTS OBSTACLES -
BOLDNESS ELIMINATES THEM.

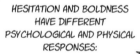

BOLDNESS REQUIRES ACTIVELY LOOKING YOUR FEARS IN THE EYE ...

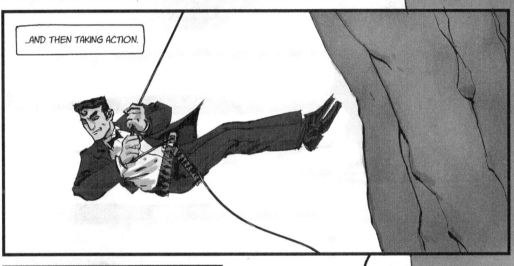

...AND THEN TAKING ACTION.

OF COURSE, YOU MIGHT STILL FAIL – BOLDNESS IS NOT THE SECRET OF SUCCESS.

BUT WITHOUT BOLDNESS, IT'S DIFFICULT TO ACHIEVE ANYTHING OF GREAT MEANING.

CHAPTER 6:
LIFE LESSONS
FROM POKER

*"YOU CAN'T PLAY POKER
NOT TO LOSE. YOU HAVE
TO PLAY TO WIN"*
-AARON BROWN

NO GAME RESEMBLES
THE COMLEXITY OF
LIFE, BUT POKER TEXAS
HOLD'EM NO LIMIT
COMES CLOSE!

HIGH-STAKES SITUATIONS IN
LIFE ARE A LOT LIKE A POKER
GAME: FAST, REQUIRING A MIX OF
SKILL, INTUITION AND LUCK.

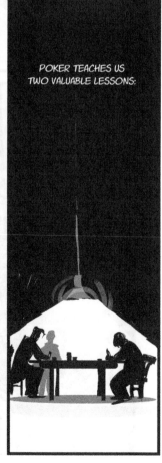

POKER TEACHES US
TWO VALUABLE LESSONS:

1: YOU CAN'T PLAY POKER NOT TO LOSE. IF YOU PLAY NOT TO LOSE (I.E. PLAY IT SAFE)...

...YOU MAKE IT IMPOSSIBLE TO WIN AND YOU'LL PROBABLY END UP LOSING. YOU HAVE TO PLAY POKER TO WIN!

2: YOU HAVE NO INFLUENCE OVER THE CARDS YOU ARE DEALT...

...BUT YOU CAN INFLUENCE THE WAY YOU PLAY YOUR CARDS.

IT'S ALL UP TO YOU TO MAKE YOUR DREAMS COME TRUE.

IN FACT, THE ACT OF SURVIVING A FALL AND GETTING UP AGAIN BUILDS CONFIDENCE.

YOU'LL FIND THAT THE SKIERS WHO FALL THE MOST CAN ALSO STAY UP THE LONGEST,

DO THE MOST TRICKS, AND SKI THE FASTEST WHEN THEY CHOOSE TO.

THE MEDIOCRE SKIER-- THE ONE WHO NEVER TRIES NEW MANEUVERS OR PUSHES HIS LIMITS - NEVER FALLS.

CHAPTER 8:
CONFIDENCE=BELIEVING IN YOURSELF

"TRUE CONFIDENCE COMES FROM THE CERTAINTY OF DOING WHATEVER IT TAKES."
- CHRISTOPHER HOWARD

WATCH ROGER FEDERER CLOSELY WHEN HE'S LOSING.

HE'S STILL PLAYING WITH THE CONFIDENCE THAT HE'S WINNING.

HE ATTACKS, ATTACKS, AND ATTACKS...

...AND NEVER THROWS IN THE TOWEL UNTIL THE GAME IS OVER.

CONFIDENCE IS YOUR PERCEPTION OF YOUR OWN POTENTIAL.

YOU MIGHT SAY: "I DON'T QUITE KNOW HOW I'M GOING TO DO IT, BUT I'M GOING TO DO IT."

CONFIDENCE IS THE SEARCH FOR WAYS TO EXECUTE THAT NEXT PLAY. HOW CAN I MAKE MY VISION A REALITY?

CLAP
CLAP
CLAP

CHAPTER 9:
A MILLION DOLLAR$

*"THE BEST PERFORMERS
IGNORE THE ODDS."
- JOHN ELLIOT, PHD*

THE CHANCES OF BECOMING SUPER SUCCESSFUL IN ANY FIELD ARE VERY LOW.

OTHERWISE, EVERYBODY WOULD BE INCREDIBLY SUCCESSFUL IN THEIR CHOSEN FIELD.

FEW THINGS IN LIFE CAN BE CALCULATED; ONE EXCEPTION IS THE STATISTICAL CHANCE OF BECOMING A MILLIONAIRE.

HERE IS AN EXAMPLE FOR THOSE OF YOU WHO LIVE IN THE USA.

THE NUMBER OF MILLIONAIRES IN THE USA (6 MILLION) / THE POPULATION OF THE USA (300 MILLION) = APPROX. 2%

SO IMAGINE 100 PEOPLE IN A ROOM. TWO WILL BECOME MILLIONAIRES. NINETY-EIGHT WILL NOT.

THAT MEANS THAT THE CHANCE OF BECOMING A MILLIONAIRE FOR A PERSON LIVING IN THE USA IS APPROXIMATELY 2%.

THE IDEA IS NOT TO GET DISCOURAGED BY THAT NUMBER, BUT TO GET ENCOURAGED!

FOLLOW YOUR DREAM - IF YOU BELIEVE IN YOUR POTENTIAL AND YOU DEVELOP THE CONFIDENCE TO FIGHT FOR WHAT YOU WANT, YOU CAN BE PART OF THAT 2%.

CHAPTER 10: BE DIFFERENT OR BE AVERAGE

"GREAT PERFORMERS ARE, BY DEFINITION, ABNORMAL."
- JOHN ELLIOT, PHD

FOR A BETTER SCIENTIFIC UNDERSTANDING, LET'S VISIT THE PSYCHOTHERAPIST, CARL JUNG.

TO BE NORMAL IS THE IDEAL OF THE UNSUCCESSFUL.

EXCEPTIONAL INDIVIDUALS ARE IMPELLED BY THEIR INNER NATURE TO SEEK THEIR OWN PATH.

AH, TO BE DIFFERENT... WE NEED TO BE ABNORMAL TO ACHIEVE ABNORMALLY.

NOT CRAZY – BUT ABNORMAL IN TERMS OF WILL, DRIVE, AND DREAMS.

BE BOLD. HAVE THE COURAGE TO BE DIFFERENT.

CHAPTER 11:
STRATEGY VS. TACTICS

*"STRATEGY IS DOING THE RIGHT THING.
TACTICS IS DOING THINGS RIGHT."*
-GERALD MICHAELSON

WE MUST UNDERSTAND
THE DIFFERENCE BETWEEN
STRATEGY AND TACTICS.

STRATEGY IS AN OVERALL
BIG-PICTURE PLAN USED TO ACHIEVE A
PARTICULAR GOAL (OR DREAM).

TACTICS ARE THE MEANS BY WHICH
YOU CARRY OUT YOUR STRATEGY.
TACTICS INCLUDE OBJECTIVES OR
STEPS TOWARDS ACHIEVING YOUR
GOAL (OR DREAM).

CHAPTER 12: FOCUS + SPEED = MOMENTUM

"CONTROLLED FOCUS IS LIKE A LASER BEAM THAT CAN CUT THROUGH ANYTHING THAT SEEMS TO BE STOPPING YOU."
- ANTHONY ROBBINS

CONNECT WITH YOUR DREAM, AND FOCUS ON WHAT IS IMPORTANT IN YOUR LIFE.

LET GO OF YOUR FEARS.

FOCUS.

FIRST THINGS FIRST.

THE REST IS (ALMOST) UNIMPORTANT IF YOU REALLY WANT TO ACHIEVE YOUR DREAM.

THE MAGIC OF THE POWER LAW LIES IN DOING THINGS WITH UNCONVENTIONAL WISDOM.

THE POWER LAW SAYS THAT 80% OF RESULTS FLOW FROM 20% OF THE CAUSES - THE ONE PRINCIPLE OF HIGHLY EFFECTIVE PEOPLE. SO FOCUS ON THE 20% THAT REALLY MATTER.

SO WHAT MATTERS? FEW THINGS REALLY MATTER IN LIFE! IN FACT, MOST ARE NOT IMPORTANT.

TO ACHIEVE YOUR DREAM, FOCUS ON THE ONE OR TWO THINGS THAT ADVANCE YOU CLOSER TO REALIZING YOUR DREAM.

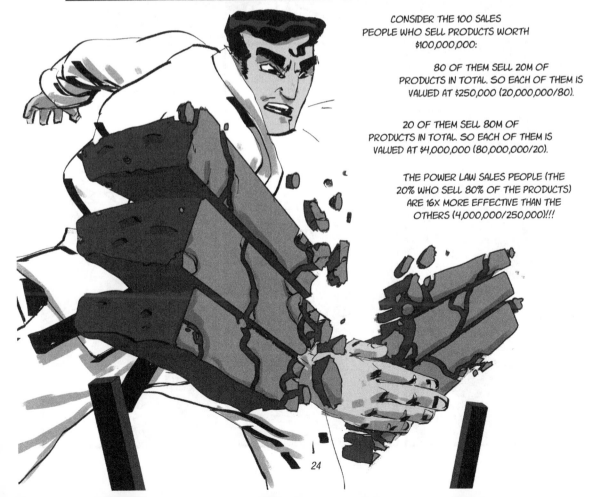

CONSIDER THE 100 SALES PEOPLE WHO SELL PRODUCTS WORTH $100,000,000:

80 OF THEM SELL 20M OF PRODUCTS IN TOTAL. SO EACH OF THEM IS VALUED AT $250,000 (20,000,000/80).

20 OF THEM SELL 80M OF PRODUCTS IN TOTAL. SO EACH OF THEM IS VALUED AT $4,000,000 (80,000,000/20).

THE POWER LAW SALES PEOPLE (THE 20% WHO SELL 80% OF THE PRODUCTS) ARE 16X MORE EFFECTIVE THAN THE OTHERS (4,000,000/250,000)!!!

CHAPTER 13:
THE AVERAGE
NEVER WINS

"THERE'S NOTHING MORE INTOXICATING
THAT DOING BIG, BOLD THINGS."
- JASON KILAR

TO BE A SUPER SUCCESSFUL INDIVIDUAL, YOU HAVE TO SEPARATE YOURSELF FROM 98% OF THE REST OF THE WORLD.

IF YOU BEHAVE LIKE ALL THE OTHERS, YOU WILL BE LIKE ALL THE OTHERS.

NORMAL OUTPUT PRODUCES NORMAL RESULTS. IN THE WORLD OF SUPERSTARS, NORMAL = NOTHING.

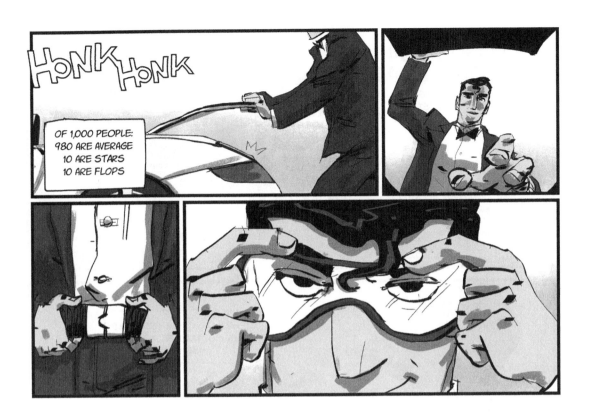

OF 1,000 PEOPLE:
980 ARE AVERAGE
10 ARE STARS
10 ARE FLOPS

YOU MUST UNDERSTAND: IF YOU DO NOT BELONG TO THE 980 AVERAGE PEOPLE, YOU ARE DESTINED TO BE EITHER A STAR OR A FLOP. THERE IS NO MIDDLE GROUND WITH BOLD PEOPLE!

IT IS ALMOST IMPOSSIBLE FOR BOLD PEOPLE TO END UP "NORMAL."

CHAPTER 14: PRISON BREAK

"FREEDOM LIES IN BEING BOLD."
- ROBERT FROST

MANY OF US HAVE BEEN TOLD BY OUR PARENTS WHAT WE CANNOT ACHIEVE.

MANY OF US HAVE BEEN TOLD BY OUR TEACHERS WHAT WE CANNOT ACHIEVE.

MANY OF US HAVE BEEN TOLD BY OUR FRIENDS WHAT WE CANNOT ACHIEVE.

MANY OF US HAVE BEEN TOLD BY OUR BOSSES WHAT WE CANNOT ACHIEVE.

BASED ON WHAT WE HAVE BEEN TOLD, WE KNOW WHAT IS IMPOSSIBLE.

BUT UNTIL WE PERMIT OURSELVES TO MOVE BEYOND THOSE LIMITATIONS, WE ARE DESTINED TO REMAIN AVERAGE.

BE BOLD.

DON'T OPERATE BASED ON LIMITATIONS IMPOSED BY OTHERS.

CHAPTER 15: CONFIDENCE PRECEDES SUCCESS

"YOU CAN DO IT IF YOU BELIEVE YOU CAN!"
- NAPOLEON HILL

OUR GREATEST LIMITATIONS ARE SELF-IMPOSED.

TO BECOME A SUPER SUCCESSFUL INDIVIDUAL, SHED YOUR SELF-IMPOSED LIMITATIONS AND BUILDCONFIDENCE IN YOURSELF.

CONFIDENCE TO GO OUT ON A LIMB.

? CONFIDENCE TO PURSUE WHAT IS NOT SAFE AND SECURE.

CONFIDENCE TO GO BOLDLY WHERE ONLY FEW DARE!

ANY LACK OF
SELF-CONFIDENCE IS
NOT OVERCOME THROUGH
CONTEMPLATION --
BUT THROUGH ACTION.

SUPERSTARS
THINK LIKE SUPERSTARS
LONG BEFORE THEY BECOME
SUPERSTARS.

CONFIDENCE
PRECEDES
SUCCESS.

MOHAMMED ALI:
"I AM THE GREATEST. I
SAID IT BEFORE I KNEW I
WAS."

DO NOT CONFUSE
CONFIDENCE WITH ARROGANCE.
CONFIDENCE IS CHOOSING THE
PATH THAT IS RIGHT FOR YOU.

ARROGANCE IS BELIEVING
YOU DESERVE THAT PATH
WITHOUT WORKING FOR IT.

IT DOESN'T
MATTER WHETHER IT'S
THE PATH TRAVELLED
BY MANY...

...OR THE PATH
TRAVELLED BY
FEW...

...OR THE PATH
TRAVELLED BY
NONE.

WHAT MATTERS IS
1) THAT IT'S YOUR OWN PATH; AND
2) THAT YOU WORK HARD FOR EVERY
STEP YOU TAKE IN THAT DIRECTION.

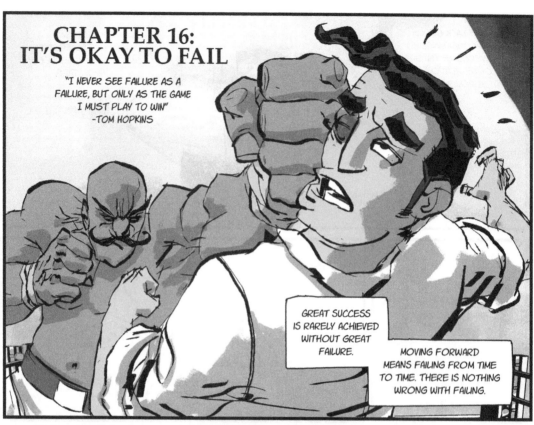

CHAPTER 16:
IT'S OKAY TO FAIL

"I NEVER SEE FAILURE AS A
FAILURE, BUT ONLY AS THE GAME
I MUST PLAY TO WIN"
-TOM HOPKINS

GREAT SUCCESS
IS RARELY ACHIEVED
WITHOUT GREAT
FAILURE.

MOVING FORWARD
MEANS FAILING FROM TIME
TO TIME. THERE IS NOTHING
WRONG WITH FAILING.

THE OPPOSITE OF SUCCESS IS
NOT FAILURE. THE OPPOSITE OF
SUCCESS IS SITTING STILL.

WHY DO WE LOOK AT FAILURE
AS THE UNTHINKABLE INSTEAD
OF REGARDING IT AMONG LIFE'S
MOST FUNDAMENTAL AND
VALUABLE EXPERIENCES?

IF YOU'VE NEVER FAILED
IN YOUR LIFE, YOU ARE
PROBABLY NOT A
DREAMER.

YOU CANNOT EMBRACE YOUR INNER BOLDNESS UNLESS YOU ARE WILLING TO MAKE MISTAKES

- EVEN WILLING TO LOOK FOOLISH OR STUPID.

HA HA HA HA HA HA

ASK YOURSELF, "WHAT DOES IT MEAN IF I FAIL?"

IF YOUR DREAM IS WORTH ACHIEVING, THE OPTION OF FAILING ON THE WAY DOES NOT LOOK SO BAD.

32

CHAPTER 17:
DARE TO BE DIFFERENT

*"ORIGINALITY IMPLIES BEING BOLD ENOUGH
TO GO BEYOND ACCEPTED NORMS."
- ANTHONY STORR*

OVERCOMING THE FEAR OF BEING DIFFERENT IS ONE OF THE DEFINING CHARACTERISTICS OF BOLD PEOPLE.

DO NOT MIND WHAT PEOPLE THINK OF YOU.

UNTIE YOURSELF FROM THE OPINIONS OF OTHERS.

THIS IS THE BASIS OF NON-CONFORMITY.

AND BEING UNIQUE MEANS YOU ARE LESSINFLUENCED BY CONVENTIONAL WISDOM AND SOCIAL EXPECTATIONS.

TO MAKE A DIFFERENCE, YOU MUST BE DIFFERENT.

FOLLOWING THE PACK IS SAFE, BUT IT IS NOT IN THE LEXICON OF SPECIAL PEOPLE.

YOU CANNOT BE EXCEPTIONAL WITHOUT BEING EXCEPTIONALLY DIFFERENT.

DO YOU WANT TO BE SPECIAL? THEN BE BOLD, AND DO THAT WHICH THE ORDINARY FEAR.

CHAPTER 18: LIFE'S A (SMART) GAMBLE

"SOMETIMES YOUR WHOLE LIFE BOILS DOWN TO ONE INSANE MOVE."
- FROM THE MOVIE AVATAR

GOING THE PATH OF A SUPERSTAR AND BELONGING TO THE TOP 2% IN YOUR FIELD REQUIRES GAMBLING ON YOURSELF.

IT IS NOT LIKE GAMBLING IN A CASINO - IT IS TAKING A LEAP OF FAITH.

BY RISKING THE KNOWN FOR THE UNKNOWN, THE FAMILIAR FOR THE UNFAMILIAR, YOU TAKE A LEAP OF FAITH THAT CANNOT BE FULLY EVALUATED OR ENTIRELY UNDERSTOOD BEFORE TAKEOFF.

DO NOT BELIEVE THOSE WHO TELL YOU THEY HAVE BECOME SUPERSTARS USING 'CALCULATED RISKS' VS. GAMBLING.

HOW CAN THEY CALCULATE RISK? NOBODY CAN CALCULATE IT!

WHETHER YOU WANT TO BECOME THE NEXT GREAT INTERNET STARTUP, REAL ESTATE TYCOON, SCIENTIST, ATHLETE OR MUSIC LEGEND, THAT KIND OF SUCCESS IS NOT SOMETHING YOU'LL THINK INTO BEING.

TAKE THE LEAP!

OF COURSE, THERE ARE SMART GAMBLES AND STUPID GAMBLES.

A STUPID GAMBLE IS ONE TAKEN WITH A BLINDFOLD ON - YOU CANNOT HIT A TARGET YOU CAN'T SEE!

BOLDNESS IS THE SMART GAMBLE - TAKEN AFTER YOU HAVE 80% OF THE INFORMATION NEEDED TO MAKE THAT DECISION, WITH A PINCH OF FAITH ADDED INTO THE MIX.

ONCE YOU'VE MADE YOUR DECISION TO CHASE YOUR DREAM, THE GAMBLE IS OFTEN THE WILLINGNESS TO INVEST ALL YOUR TIME AND MONEY IN MAKING THAT DREAM A REALITY.

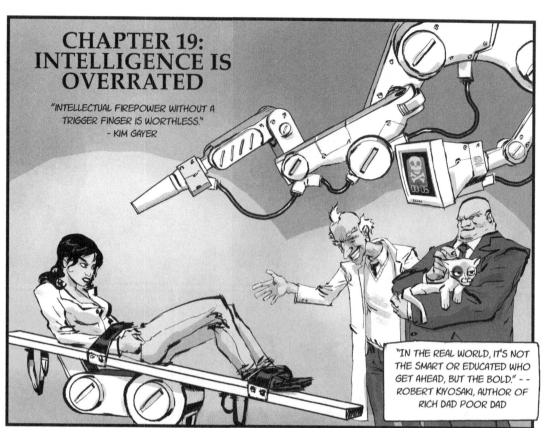

CHAPTER 19: INTELLIGENCE IS OVERRATED

"INTELLECTUAL FIREPOWER WITHOUT A TRIGGER FINGER IS WORTHLESS."
- KIM GAYER

"IN THE REAL WORLD, IT'S NOT THE SMART OR EDUCATED WHO GET AHEAD, BUT THE BOLD." - - ROBERT KIYOSAKI, AUTHOR OF RICH DAD POOR DAD

WHY ARE IQ TESTS STILL POPULAR?

OUTSIDE OF SCHOOLS AND UNIVERSITIES, RARELY DOES THE MAN WITH AN IQ OF 125 BEAT THE MAN WITH AN IQ OF 115 IN THE GAME OF LIFE.

WORLD-CLASS PERFORMANCE IN MOST COMPETITIVE FIELDS OFTEN HAS LITTLE TO DO WITH SCORES ON TESTS AND MORE TO DO WITH BEHAVIOR.

SUPERSTARS ARE NORMAL PEOPLE WHEN IT COMES TO GENETICS, ...

... BUT THEY ARE ARMED WITH BOLDNESS.

BOLDNESS IS A BEHAVIOR...

AND NO MINIMUM IQ NUMBER IS REQUIRED TO DEMONSTRATE BOLDNESS.

CHAPTER 21: BOLD DECISIONS

"DON'T WASTE TIME FANTASIZING ABOUT A WORLD OF PERFECT CHOICES."
- MARCUS AURELIUS

IF A DECISION HAS TO BE MADE, DON'T HESITATE - MAKE IT.

IN REAL LIFE, THERE IS NO PERFECT TIME FOR ANYTHING. PERFECTION IS STATIC, BUT LIFE IS DYNAMIC AND THEREFORE IMPERFECT BY ITS DEFINITION.

MANY OF OUR PROBLEMS TODAY ARE NOT THE RESULT OF TOO LITTLE INFORMATION BUT OF TOO MUCH INFORMATION.

WE HAVE TO STOP DROWNING IN INFORMATION AND DETERMINE WHAT IS REALLY IMPORTANT.

THIS FORCES US TO BE SMART BECAUSE WE HAVE TO USE WHAT WE KNOW.

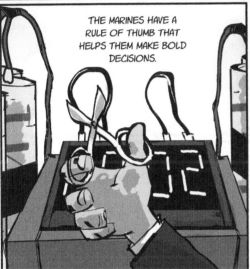

THE MARINES HAVE A RULE OF THUMB THAT HELPS THEM MAKE BOLD DECISIONS.

THE RULE SAYS THAT ONCE YOU HAVE OBTAINED 80% OF THE INFORMATION YOU NEED TO MAKE A DECISION, ...

SNAP

...ANY FURTHER DELAY SIMPLY BECOMES HESITATION.

CHAPTER 22: HIGH-STAKES NEGOTIATION

"A BOLD HEART IS HALF THE BATTLE."
- ANONYMOUS

MANY OF THE DAILY SITUATIONS WE FIND OURSELVES IN DON'T REQUIRE BOLD NEGOTIATION TACTICS - IN PARTICULAR, SITUATIONS WITH FAMILY AND FRIENDS.

BUT IN HIGH-STAKES SITUATIONS, YOU WANT TO BE READY TO NEGOTIATE WELL.

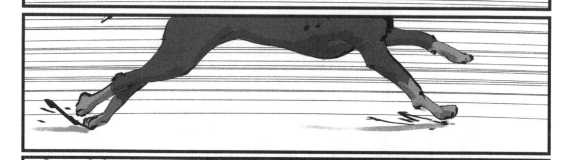

NEGOTIATION TAKES A LOT OF PRACTICE - SO TRY TO IMPROVE YOUR NEGOTIATION SKILLS AS FREQUENTLY AS POSSIBLE.

LOW-STAKES NEGOTIATIONS ARE GOOD EXERCISES TO PREPARE FOR HIGH-STAKES SITUATIONS.

THE TWO BASIC RULES OF BOLD NEGOTIATIONS:

1 – NEVER EVER ACCEPT THE FIRST OFFER

NEGOTIATORS EXPECT TO NEGOTIATE. IF YOU ACCEPT THE FIRST PRICE, YOU OFTEN INSULT THE OTHER PARTY.

WHILE YOU MIGHT THINK THEY WOULD BE HAPPY WITH YOUR ACCEPTANCE, THEY OFTEN FEEL UPSET BY IT.

WHY? BECAUSE THEY ARE LEFT THINKING THAT THEY COULD HAVE GOTTEN MUCH MORE!

2 – YOUR OPENING MUST BE SHOCKING

IF YOU'RE BUYING, SHOCK 'EM WITH YOUR OFFER AND GO AS LOW AS YOU CAN WHILE STILL MAKING IT CREDIBLE WITHOUT SOUNDING SILLY.

SHOCKING OFFERS - PROVIDED THEY ARE CREDIBLE - LEAVE YOU LOTS OF ROOM TO NEGOTIATE.

CHAPTER 23: THINK TWICE, BUT GO WITH YOUR GUT

"THE VERY ESSENCE OF INSTINCT IS THAT IT'S FOLLOWED INDEPENDENTLY OF REASON."
– CHARLES DARWIN

AS WE DECIDE AND CHOOSE, OUR DESTINIES ARE FORMED.

WHEN IT COMES TO DECISION MAKING, YOU'LL GET THE BEST RESULTS BY MIXING CRITICAL THINKING AND INTUITIVE THINKING.

CRITICAL THINKING IS DRAWN FROM THE LEFT HEMISPHERE OF THE BRAIN. IT IS BASED ON FACTS AND LOGIC. ALWAYS THINK TWICE.

OUR BRAINS DON'T LIKE TO THINK TWICE - IT TAKES EFFORT - BUT OFTEN THE WORST MISTAKES CAN BE AVOIDED BY THINKING TWICE.

INTUITIVE THINKING IS DRAWN FROM THE RIGHT HIMISPHERE OF THE BRAIN.

IT IS KNOWING SOMETHING WITHOUT BEING ABLE TO EXPLAIN HOW YOU CAME TO YOUR CONLUSION.

IT'S A MYSTERIOUS GUT FEELING OR INSTINCT THAT CAN SOLVE PROBLEMS YOU CAN'T SOLVE WITH YOUR BRAIN.

WITHOUT INTUITION, WE WOULD BE NOTHING MORE THAN COMPUTERS.

THINK, THINK AGAIN, AND THEN GO WITH YOUR GUT FEELING.

CHAPTER 24:
MAKE LUCK WOR
FOR YOU

"A BOLD GENERAL MAY BE LUCKY, BUT ON GENERAL CAN BE LUCKY UNLESS HE IS BOLD."
—GENERAL WAVELL

NO SUPERSTAR DISDAINS LUCK. BUT NO SUPERSTAR DEPENDS ON IT EITHER!

TO A CERTAIN DEGREE, LUCK CAN BE ACTIVELY INFLUENCED.

"A POSITIVE ATTITUDE TOWARD LUCK MEANS BEING READY FOR IT, SPOTTING IT, AND MAKING THE MAXIMUM USE OF IT, VS. SITTING AROUND WAITING FOR IT."
—EDWARD DE BONO

UNDERSTAND LUCK, AND MAKE IT WORK FOR YOU.

PSYCHOLOGICALLY, WINNERS UNDERSTAND THAT GOOD LUCK IS A MANUFACTURED ARTICLE.

SO THEY THINK IN TERMS OF GOOD THINGS HAPPENING TO THEM AND MAKE THEMSELVES GOOD-LUCK-PRONE.

BY THINKING ABOUT BEING THE RECIPIENT OF BAD LUCK, YOUR SUBCONSCIOUS MIND CAN GET CONFUSED AND BEGIN ACTING LIKE BAD LUCK IS WHAT YOU WANT TO HAVE HAPPEN.

ALWAYS MAKE YOUR SUBCONSCIOUS MIND WORK FOR YOU.

CHAPTER 25:
GO FOR A HOMERUN

*"I AM NOT JUDGED BY THE NUMBER OF
TIMES I FAIL, BUT BY THE NUMBER OF
TIMES I SUCCEED".
-TOM HOPKINS*

CONSISTENCY IN LIFE IS OFTEN A
GOOD THING, BUT IT IS NOT ALWAYS
OPTIMAL. FORGET CONSISTENCY IF
YOU WANT TO SWING FOR A HOME RUN.

THE SUPERSTAR BASEBALL PLAYERS
ARE THE HOMERUN HITTERS - NOT
THOSE WITH CONSISTENT BATTING
RECORDS.

CLACK

BABE RUTH, AN AMERICAN
BASEBALL PLAYER, PERFECTLY
SUMMARIZED HOW TO HIT
HOME RUNS: "I SWING BIG,
WITH EVERYTHING I'VE GOT. I
HIT BIG OR I MISS BIG. I LIKE
TO LIVE AS BIG AS I CAN."

NOTES & REFERENCES

CHAPTER 1: LIVE YOUR DREAMS

Overachievement: The New Science of Working Less to Accomplish More by John Eliot (Portfolio Trade, 2006)

If you want to be the best in anything, this is the most comprehensive psychology book in the world. Chapter 4 approaches dreams scientifi cally for anyone who wants to rise above what you ever thought possible.

MIND GYM by Gary Mack with David Casstevens (McGraw Hill, 2001)

This book is a winner; it's an athlete's guide to inner excellence. On page 184, the author explains the philosophy of being quick but never in a hurry.

The Magic of Thinking Big by David J. Schwartz (Pocket Books, 1979)

The all-time classic book on thinking BIG. Chapter 5: 'How to Think and Dream Creatively' shows how your mind can help make your dreams come true.

CHAPTER 2: YOUR DAYS ARE NUMBERED

The 33 Strategies of War by Robert Greene (Profile Books, 2006)

With examples from the philosophies of the ancient Samurai, Robert Greene states brilliantly how the illusion of limitless time comes with a terrible price (page 47).

CHAPTER 3: LIFE IS RISKY

All the Money in the World: How the Forbes 400 Make—and Spend—Their Fortunes by Peter Bernstein and Annalyn Swan's (Knopf, 2007)

In the chapter titled Risk, the author demonstrates that many Forbes 400 individuals have been willing to take gargantuan risks in order to realize their dreams.

Courage: The Joy of Living Dangerously by Osho (St. Martin's Griffin, 1999)
A book about courage that shows there can be no security in life.

CHAPTER 4: ACCEPT YOUR FEARS, BUT DO IT ANYWAY

"There is a time to take counsel of your fears, and there is a time to never listen to any fear. It is always important to know exactly what you are doing. The time to take counsel of your fears is before you make an important battle decision. That is the time to listen to every fear you can imagine! When you have collected all of the facts and fears, make your decision. After you make your decision, forget all of your fears and go full steam ahead."
George S. Patton

PATTON ON LEADERSHIP by Alan Axelrod (Prentice Hall Press, 1999)

To me, no book is more applicable to General Patton's thoughts on leadership. Page 79 is all about fear and knowing exactly what you are doing.

How to Master the Art of Selling by Tom Hopkins (Grand Central Publishing, 1988)

One of the best books I've ever read. Although the book is focused on sales, the main thesis is simply that champions are made, not born. Many people are scared of failing (in sales), but it isn't failure that hurts us most. Fear of failure does the greatest damage, and we have to learn to overcome our fear if we want to accomplish great things.

CHAPTER 5: BOLD ACTION OR NO ACTION

The 48 Laws of Power by Robert Greene (Profi le Books, 2000)

Robert Greene includes boldness as a law in his book: LAW 28 – ENTER ACTION WITH BOLDNESS.

The Art of Seduction by Robert Greene (Penguin, 2003)

Chapter 23, Master the Art of the Bold Move, shows how the charismatic seducer can use boldness to his or her advantage.

CHAPTER 6: LIFE LESSONS FROM POKER

Rich Dad, Poor Dad by Robert T. Kiyosaki (BUSINESS PLUS, 1997)

In my favorite personal fi nance book, Robert T. Kiyosaki explains how 'playing not to lose' can have disastrous outcomes (page 194).

All the Money in the World: How the Forbes 400 Make – and Spend – Their Fortunes by Peter W. Bernstein and Annalyn Swan (Knopf, 2007)

The authors show in Chapter 2 (Risk) how some Forbes 400 members had to take gigantic risks. Not surprisingly, many were passionate poker players early in their careers.

CHAPTER 7: LIFE LESSONS FROM SKIING

The Innovative Mind by Gene N. Landrum, PhD. (Morgan James Publishing, 2008)

Gene N. Landrum shows beautifully that skiing is not that different from learning to launch a new business, learning to fly, or learning to deal with the vagaries of life (Page 132 – 133).

CHAPTER 8: CONFIDENCE = BELIEVING IN YOURSELF

Overachievement: The New Science of Working Less to Accomplish More by John Eliot (Portfolio Trade, 2006)

There is no better treatise in the world about the 'Science of the Confidence Habit' for super performers than in chapter 7.

CHAPTER 9: A MILLION DOLLAR$

Head First Statistics by David Griffiths (O'Reilly, 2009) – chapter 11, page 45

This example is based on the statistical concept that probability and proportion are related. The proportion of success (2% in our example), is exactly the same as the probability of being successful (becoming a millionaire).

Taking Chances: Winning with Probability by John Haigh (OXFORD University Press, 1999)

John Haigh shows mathematically that in unfavorable games, bold play is best, and timid play is worst.

CHAPTER 10: BE DIFFERENT OR BE AVERAGE

The Outsiders Edge by Brent D. Taylor (John Wiley & Sons Australia, 2007)

Brent D. Taylor uses a sample of 17 self–made billionaires to explain why they're outsiders and how they found the edge that has led them to extreme wealth.

The Superman Syndrome – The Magic of Myth in The Pursuit of Power: The Positive Mental Moxie of Myth for Personal Growth by Gene N. Landrum, PhD. (iUniverse, 2005)

Dr. Landrum provides scientific insight into those who are different (page 179).

CHAPTER 11: STRATEGY vs. TACTICS

"Have been giving everyone a simplified directive of war. Use steamroller strategy; that is, make up your mind on course and direction of action, and stick to it. But in tactics, do not steamroller. Attack weakness."
General Patton

PATTON ON LEADERSHIP by Alan Axelrod (Prentice Hall Press, 1999)
Alan Axelrod writes brilliantly in his book how to apply the ideas of Patton on steamrolling (page 57).

The 33 Strategies of War by Robert Greene (Profi le Books, 2006)
Timeless strategies and tactics of war apply to business and life. This is the all–in–one book on military genius's, including Alexander, Patton, Hannibal, Napoleon, Clausewitz, and more. Studying those men can greatly help you in strategic and tactical thinking.

How Life Imitates Chess: Making the Right Moves, from the Board to the Boardroom by Garry Kasparov (Bloomsbury, 2007)
Kasparov is world famous for being a very aggressive chess player. And when the greatest chess player of our times writes about THE ATTACKER'S ADVANTAGE, we should pay attention.

Game Theory at Work: How to Use Game Theory to Outthink and Outmaneuver Your Competition by James D. Miller (McGraw–Hill, 2003)
Game Theory is the formalized study of strategy – how competitors act, react, and interact in their strategic pursuit of self–interest. If you want to buy only one book on the subject of strategy, this one is best.

Thinking Strategically: The Competitive Edge in Business, Politics and Everyday Life by Avinash K. Dixit and Barry J. Nalebuff (W.W. Norton & Co., 1993)
A non–technical book with case studies taken from business, sports, the movies, politics, and gambling. This book can make you a smarter strategist in life.

On War by Carl von Clausewitz (Penguin Books, 1968)
First published in German (titled 'Vom Kriege') in 1832, this book is probably the most important book on military strategy ever written. From the transport driver and the drummer, all the way up to the General, Clausewitz calls boldness the noblest of all virtues (Chapter VI: BOLDNESS).

CHAPTER 12: FOCUSE + SPEED = MOMENTUM

The 80/20 Principles: The Secret of Success to Achieving More with Less by Richard Koch (Nicholas Brealy Publishing, 1998)
Probably the best book on the 80/20 Principle (a.k.a. the Power Law).

Warfighting: U.S. Marine Corps Staff (CURRENCY DOUBLEDAY, 1994)
A brilliant chapter on Concentration and Speed (page 39).

The 7 Habits of Highly Effective People by Stephen R. Covey (Simon & Schuster, 1990)
This is my personal favorite of self–help books. Habit 3, Put First Things First, is about the widespread addiction to urgency instead of importance.

CHAPTER 13: THE AVERAGE NEVER WINS

Profiles of Genius: Thirteen Creative Men Who Changed the World by Gene N. Landrum, PhD. (Prometheus Books, 1996)
I developed the concept of 'The Average Never Wins' during my time on the trading floors around the world; Dr. Landrum wrote about the same concept in 'Abnormality & Success' (page 37).

Rich Dad, Poor Dad by Robert T. Kiyosaki (BUSINESS PLUS, 1997)
Robert Kiyosaki observes something similar in this great book: balanced people go nowhere.

FUNKY BUSINESS FOREVER by Jonas Ridderstrale & Kjell Norstrom (FT Prentice Hall, 2000)
One of my favorite business books postulates several great messages throughout the book, including 'The Average Never Wins.'

CHAPTER 14: PRISON BREAK

The topic has been covered widely – from Greek philosopher Plato to today's best books and movies, including 'V for Vendetta' and 'The Matrix.'

The 50th Law by 50 Cent and Robert Greene (Harper Studio, 2009)
The book explains that our fears are a kind of prison and tells how to break out of it.

CHAPTER 15: CONFIDENCE PRECEDES SUCCESS

Overachievement: The New Science of Working Less to Accomplish More by John Eliot (Portfolio Trade, 2006)

I strongly believe that if you want to become a superstar in any field, this is the best 'peak performance book' in the world. Dr. Eliot draws on both cutting–edge research in cognitive neuroscience and his real–world coaching of Olympic athletes, surgeons, actors, salespeople, and superstars in other fields. Chapter 7 is all about confidence for champions.

CHAPTER 16: IT'S OK TO FAIL

How to Master the Art of Selling by Tom Hopkins (Grand Central Publishing, 1988)

Here you'll find the best advice I have ever read on how to cope with failure in the context of selling and how the advice applies to any human endeavor (pages 110–123).

Overachievement: The New Science of Working Less to Accomplish More by John Eliot (Portfolio Trade, 2006)

Pages 238 – 244 discuss 'failure' in high performance.

CHAPTER 17: DARE TO BE DIFFERENT

How to be Rich by J. Paul Getty (Jove, 1986)

The chapter 'The Art of Individuality' must have inspired millions around the world. Getty advocates on individuality – how you need to be different from the others around you to be successful.

The Portable Jung by Editor Joseph Campbell (Penguin, 1976)

The most comprehensive collection of writings by the epoch shaping Swiss psychoanalyst.

The Superman Syndrome – The Magic of Myth in The Pursuit of Power: The Positive Mental Moxie of Myth for Personal Growth by Gene N. Landrum, PhD. (iUniverse, 2005)

Dr. Landrum describes the "superman syndrome" as a series of common behaviors that permit an otherwise average person to rise above the norm. He points out that some of the world's most renowned visionaries – Catherine the Great, Walt Disney, and Ian Fleming – did not conform to tradition because they modeled their behavior on heroic ideals and mythical mentors.

The 33 Strategies of War by Robert Greene (Profi le Books, 2006)

On page 323, Robert Greene writes brilliantly about the price we have to pay for conformity.

CHAPTER 18: LIFE'S A (SMART) GAMBLE

The Poker Face of Wall Street by Aaron Brown (Wiley, 2006)

During my years on several trading floors around the world, everybody was talking about how to manage and calculate risk, while Aaron Brown was writing about 'The Art of Uncalculated Risk.' Uncalculated risk! He changed the way I look at risk forever.

The Innovative Mind by Gene N. Landrum, PhD. (Morgan James Publishing, 2008)

This book aims to help readers change from followers to leaders, offering insights into what it takes to become more innovative and to bet what you have to get what you want (page 205).

Entrepreneurial Genius: The Power of Passion by Gene N. Landrum, PhD. (Brendan Kelly Publishing, 2004)

If you want to understand what makes an entrepreneur tick, I highly recommend this book. It's not simply the biographies of successful entrepreneurs. Rather, it's a composite psychobiography which analyzes the motivations and personality traits that characterize those entrepreneurs. Dr. Landrum writes extensively about the ability to take risk (page 354).

Taking Chances: Winning with Probability by John Haigh (OXFORD University Press, 1999)

This book can help improve your 'smart gambling' skills and explains you why bold play means making as few bets as possible (page 196).

CHAPTER 19: INTELLIGENCE IS OVERRATED

It's Not How Good You Are, It's How Good You Want to Be by Paul Arden (Phaidon Press, 2003)

A fantastic book of how to succeed in the world – a pocket 'bible' for the talented and timid to make the unthinkable thinkable and the impossible possible.

Profiles of Power & Success by Gene N. Landrum, Ph.D. (Prometheus Books, 1996)

Many books have been written about the subject of intelligence and talent, but few can match Dr. Landrum's deep understanding of what makes super successful people tick (page 40 and 41).

Rich Dad, Poor Dad by Robert T. Kiyosaki (BUSINESS PLUS, 1997)

Often, it's not the smart that get ahead but the bold (page 140).

De Bono's Thinking Course by Edward de Bono (BBC Books, 1982)

This is an excellent observation on how intelligent people can be caught in 'The Intelligence Trap' because they can defend poor ideas so well (page 12).

CHAPTER 20: IGNORANCE CAN BE SMART

The Black Swan by Nassim Taleb (Random House, 2007)

Rightly named by Fortune as 'one of the smartest books of all the time,' Taleb writes like no other about the toxicity of knowledge – or why more information is not always better (page 145).

CHAPTER 21: BOLD DECISIONS

The Marine Corps Way by Jason A. Santamaria, Vincent Martino, and Eric K. Clemons, PhD. (McGraw Hill, 2004)

Chapter 5 on BOLDNESS is an excellent description of how to apply boldness in business using the 80% rule the Marine way.

CHAPTER 22: HIGH-STAKES NEGOTIATIONS

Getting to Yes by Roger Fisher & William Ury (Arrow Books Limited, 1981)

I believe this book should have received the Nobel Peace Prize. It shows that there is an alternative way to negotiate—neither hard nor soft, but rather a combination of hard and soft.

Everything is Negotiable by Gavin Kennedy (RANDOM HOUSE BUSINESS, 1997)

This is the most extraordinary book on negotiation strategy and tactics available. Pages 103, 107, and 109 are all about toughness in negotiation.

CHAPTER 23: THINK TWICE, BUT GO WITH YOUR GUT

Think BIG and Kick Ass in Business and Life by Donald J. Trump and Bill Zanker (Collins Business, 2007)

Chapter 3, BASIC INSTINCTS, is an excellent chapter on blending logic and instinct.

Think Twice by Michael J. Mauboussin (Harvard Business Press, 2009)

An excellent book on cognitive mistakes, keeping our intuition in check, and why thinking twice is unnatural to us.

Head First Data Analysis: A Learner's Guide to Big Numbers, Statistics, and Good Decisions by Michael Milton (O'Reilly Media, 2009)

A difficult topic well explained: 'Subjective Probabilities' and how to inject some rigor in our hunches (Chapter 7, page 191).

De Bono's Thinking Course by Edward de Bono (BBC Books, 1982)

In Chapter 8 (gut feeling and thinking), Edward De Bono illustrates the dangers of "gut feeling" as a substitute for thinking.

CHAPTER 24: MAKE LUCK WORK FOR YOU

Tactics: The Art and Science of Success by Edward de Bono (Profile Books, 1985)
One of the great revolutionary thinkers of our time on success. The positive attitude toward luck page 17.

Think BIG and Kick Ass in Business and Life by Donald J. Trump and Bill Zanker (Collins Business, 2007)
Donald Trump explains in the chapter, CREATING LUCK, how to prepare for luck and how to run with it.

CHAPTER 25: GO FOR A HOME RUN

Trump: The Art of the Comeback by Donald Trump (Crown Business, 1997)
Donald Trump tells how he swings for the fences and how some big swings go sour but result in grand slams.

More Than You Know: Finding Financial Wisdom in Unconventional Places by Michael J. Mauboussin (Columbia University Press, 2008)
Michael J. Mauboussin writes about the 'The Babe Ruth Effect' and how the frequency of correctness does not matter; it is the magnitude of correctness that matters.

Please visit www.smartercomics.com/quiz for the answers and more quizzes.

Q: If you never try something new:

    A. You might still succeed.
    B. You make it impossible to succeed.
    C. You will never fail.

Q: Should you be fearless?

    A. No, but don't listen to your fears.
    B. Yes, fearlessness allows you to achieve anything in life.
    C. No, you should listen to your fears but have the courage to face them if necessary.

Q: Confidence is all about:

    A. Your perception of your own potential.
    B. Believing in yourself.
    C. Telling everybody how great you are.

Q: The chance of having $1,000,000 in your bank account in the U.S.A. is:

    A. 20.00%
    B. 2.00%
    C. 0.20%

Q: Strategy allows you to think:

    A. Long–term.
    B. Short–term.
    C. Both long–term and short–term.

Q: Is it okay to fail from time to time?

    A. Yes, great success is rarely achieved without great failure.
    B. No, successful people don't fail.
    C. No, only losers fail.

Q: Does an IQ of 125 always beat an IQ of 115?

    A. A higher IQ does not necessarily beat a lower IQ.
    B. A higher IQ always beats a lower IQ.
    C. A higher IQ means I'm smarter.

Q: Intuitive thinking (your gut feeling) is drawn from which part of the brain?

    A. The left hemisphere.
    B. The right hemisphere.
    C. Both the left and right hemispheres.

Q: One of the biggest mistakes in negotiations is:

    A. Preparing too much.
    B. Accepting the first offer.
    C. Not being aggressive enough.

Q: If you fail while following your dream:

    A. You should give up.
    B. You should change your dream.
    C. You shouldn't care about temporary setbacks.

ABOUT THE AUTHOR

Franco Arda is the CEO and founder of SmarterComics. Born in Switzerland, he earned his MBA in the UK, then worked in derivatives sales for Deutsche Bank, an investment bank in London, Zurich, and Hong Kong. In spring 2008, feeling the need for change, he left the banking industry. Fortune Favors the Bold was written to inspire his daughter's success in life. Not being satisfied with a text-based book, he met with a comic artist, Anjin Anhut, and the idea of SmarterComics was born.

Other titles from
SmarterComics™

SHUT UP, STOP WHINING & GET A LIFE from SmarterComics
By Larry Winget

Internationally renowned success philosopher, business speaker, and humorist, Larry Winget offers advice that flies in the face of conventional self–help. SHUT UP, STOP WHINING, AND GET A LIFE forces all responsibility for every aspect of your life right where it belongs: on you.

THE ART OF WAR from SmarterComics
By Sun Tzu

Written by an ancient Chinese military general and philosopher, THE ART OF WAR reveals the subtle secrets of successful competition – equally applicable to war, business, politics, sports, law, poker, gaming, and life. Required reading in modern business schools!

THINK & GROW RICH from SmarterComics
By Napoleon Hill

The comic book that could make you rich … Think and Grow Rich has sold over 30 million copies and is regarded as the greatest wealth–building guide of all time. Read this comic version and cut to the heart of the message!

MI BARRIO from SmarterComics
by Robert J. Renteria, Jr.

"Don't let where you came from dictate who you are, but let it be part of who you become." That's the message of MI BARRIO, the memoir of a man who slept in a dresser drawer as a child and grew up to become a civic leader, business owner, and VP of a publicly traded company. This hard–hitting tale, written in English, is used in schools to battle gangs, school violence, and the dropout rate.

THE LONG TAIL from SmarterComics
by Chris Anderson

Now in comic format, this 2006 New York Times bestseller introduced the business world to a future that's already here. It explains why the focus of Internet commerce is not on hits but on misses–the long tail of the demand curve – and illuminates the reasons behind the success of niche operations like Amazon.com, iTunes, and Netflix. A must–read for every entrepreneur and manager.

OVERACHIEVEMENT from SmarterComics
by Dr. John Eliot

In OVERACHIEVEMENT from SmarterComics, Dr. Eliot offers the rest of us the unconventional and counterintuitive concepts embraced by Olympic athletes, business moguls, rock stars, top surgeons, salespeople, and financial experts who have turned to him for performance–enhancement advice. Says George Foreman, entrepreneur and former world–champion boxer: "This book delivers a knockout punch. If you want to succeed in business, read it."

HOW TO MASTER THE ART OF SELLING from SmarterComics
by Tom Hopkins

A national bestseller, with over one million copies sold in its original version, this book is a classic for teaching the tools of selling success. Lauded by motivational icon Zig Ziglar, the author has been called "America's #1 sales trainer."

www.smartercomics.com

CPSIA information can be obtained at www.ICGtesting.com
Printed in the USA
BVOW10s1325231213

339914BV00009B/384/P